Cambridge Discovery Readers

Starter Level

Series editor: Nicholas Tims

Quick Change!

Margaret Johnson

GW00504623

CAMBRIDGE
UNIVERSITY PRESS

CAMBRIDGE UNIVERSITY PRESS
Cambridge, New York, Melbourne, Madrid, Cape Town, Singapore,
São Paulo, Delhi

Cambridge University Press
Basílica 17, 28020 Madrid, Spain

www.cambridge.org
Information on this title: www.cambridge.org/9788483238097

First published 2010

Printed in Spain by Gráficas Varona, S.A.

ISBN 978-84-832-3809-7 Paperback; legal deposit: S.148-2010
ISBN 978-84-832-3756-4 Paperback with audio CD/CD-ROM pack for Windows,
Mac and Linux; legal deposit: S.149-2010

No character in this work is based on any person living or dead.
Any resemblance to an actual person or situation is purely accidental.

Illustrations by Sebastijan Camagajevac (Beehive Illustration)

Editorial management by hyphen

Audio recording by BraveArts, S.L.

Exercises by hyphen

The publishers are grateful to the following for permission to reproduce
photographic material:

Steven Puetzer | Getty Images for cover image

The paper that this book has been printed on is produced using an elemental
chlorine free (ECF) process at mills registered to ISO14001 (2004), the
environmental management standard. The mills source their wood fibre from
sustainable forests. No hardwood pulp is used in the production of this paper.

Contents

People in the story

Helen: a twelve-year-old girl
Mum: Helen's mother
Dad: Helen's father
Auntie Carol: Helen's aunt
Joe: a bad man
Frank: another bad man

BEFORE YOU READ

1 Look at the pictures in Chapter 1 and *People in the story*. What do you think? Answer the questions.

1 What does Helen's dad drive?

2 Is the baby Helen?

My twelfth birthday

Listen. I've got an interesting story. It's about me. Where do I start?

OK, I know. My birthday. My twelfth birthday. My mother and father want to talk to me.

My mum and dad smile a lot. They're happy people. But they aren't smiling today.

'We love you, Helen,' Mum tells me.

'Yes,' Dad says. 'We love you very much.'

'But, Helen … we must tell you something,' Mum says.
I look at Mum. I don't understand.

'*What?*' I say.

Dad holds my hand. He looks into my eyes.

'We love you, Helen. You're our daughter. But … you're our adoptive[1] daughter.'

There is a noise in my ears. Someone's shouting. It's me.

'*No!*'

'Please, Helen,' Mum says.

Dad takes something from the table and gives it to me.
'Please. Read this,' he says.

'I'm driving the taxi when I hear something. Something in the taxi. I stop to look. And I see you.'

He smiles. 'You're crying and you're angry. But you're very beautiful too. Just one look, Helen. One look and I love you.'

I look at them.

'But who am I?' I ask. 'Who are my …'

'Your birth parents?' Dad says sadly. 'We don't know. No one knows.'

He gives me something. 'This is yours, Helen,' he says. 'I think it comes from … them.'

I look at it. 'From my birth parents?' I ask.

'Yes.'

'What is it?' I ask.

'A baby blanket,' he tells me.

Mum takes my hand now. 'Please don't be sad,' she says. 'We love you, Helen. We aren't your birth parents, but that doesn't change anything.'

But she's wrong.

LOOKING BACK

1 Check your answers to *Before you read* on page 4.

ACTIVITIES

2 Complete the sentences about Chapter 1 with the names in the box.

> Helen (x3)　　Mum (x2)　　Dad　　Mum and Dad

1 It's *Helen* 's birthday.
2 .... is twelve today.
3 Helen doesn't understand what her .... says.
4 .... is shouting.
5 .... gives Helen a baby blanket.
6 .... love Helen.
7 .... is wrong.

3 Who do the <u>underlined</u> words refer to in these lines from the text?

1 <u>They</u>'re happy people. (page 5) *Mum and Dad*
2 But <u>they</u> aren't smiling today. (page 5) ....
3 <u>He</u> smiles. (page 7) ....
4 I look at <u>them</u>. (page 8) ....
5 'I think it comes from ... <u>them</u>.' (page 8) ....
6 'Please don't be sad,' <u>she</u> says. (page 9) ....

10

4 Underline the correct words in each sentence.

1 This is an interesting story about *Helen* / *Helen's mum and dad*.

2 Helen hears a noise in her *head* / *ears*.

3 *Helen* / *Dad* reads about the baby.

4 Helen's dad finds a baby *in* / *behind* the taxi.

5 Helen's mum and dad *know* / *don't know* about her birth parents.

6 Dad *looks* / *doesn't look* happy when Helen asks about her birth parents.

7 The baby blanket is from Helen's *birth parents* / *adoptive parents*.

5 Match the questions with the answers.

1 Why is today an interesting day for Helen? ☐ *6*

2 Who isn't smiling? ☐

3 What is Helen doing in the taxi? ☐

4 Why is Helen's dad sad? ☐

5 What does Helen's dad give her? ☐

a She's crying.

~~b~~ It's her twelfth birthday.

c A baby blanket.

d Helen's mum and dad.

e He doesn't know about her birth parents.

LOOKING FORWARD

6 Tick (✓) what you think happens in Chapter 2.

1 Helen finds her birth parents. ☐

2 Helen doesn't find her birth parents. ☐

Chapter 2

A bed

I look at the baby blanket often. I look at Mum and Dad too. They're dark. I'm not. They're tall. I'm not. They like going out all the time. I like being at home. They like doing things. I like thinking. I like looking out of my window and … just thinking.

Mum and Dad often smile at me. 'What are you thinking about, Helen?' they ask. I know they love me, but they don't understand me. And then I think about my birth parents and I feel very sad. Who am I?

We live in a flat. Mum and Dad drive taxis – that's their job. The taxi office is below our flat.

Mum and Dad are often working. Auntie Carol, my mum's sister, works in the taxi office. People call for a taxi and she answers the phone. I often sit with Auntie Carol in the office. She's funny. I laugh a lot with her.

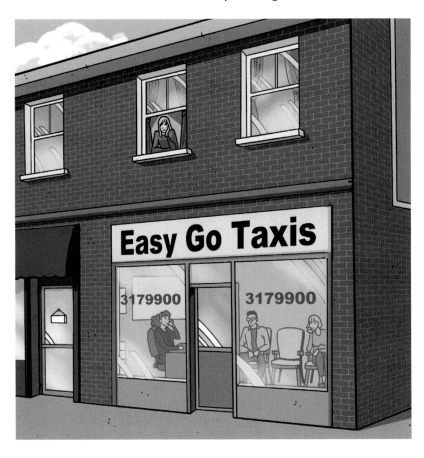

Three days after my twelfth birthday, Auntie Carol
is working in the office. I am in my room in our flat.
Auntie Carol calls up to me.

'Helen? Are you coming down?'

She must know about the baby in the taxi story. But
I don't want to talk to her about it. I get into bed.

I close my eyes. I don't want to talk to Auntie Carol. I don't.

The window is open and it's cold in my room. But I'm not cold. My head feels hot. And my hands feel hot too. I look at them. They're … yellow. *Yellow*!

Then I hear a voice[2] in my head. I don't know if the voice is a man or a woman. 'Put your hands on the bed,' the voice says. 'You can *be* the bed!'

Who is talking to me? I don't understand, but I put my hands on the bed. 'I am the bed,' I think. 'I *am* the bed!'

Then … this is very strange[3]. I start to change! I look at my hands and they aren't hands. I look at my legs and they aren't legs. I'm not Helen now. I am the bed!

How am I a bed? I don't know. Why am I a bed? I don't know. I just know I am. I am the bed and the bed is me!

LOOKING BACK

1 Check your answers to *Looking forward* on page 11.

ACTIVITIES

2 <u>Underline</u> the correct words in each sentence.
1 Helen looks at the blanket *a lot* / *very little*.
2 Helen is *tall* / *short*.
3 Helen *likes* / *doesn't like* going out all the time.
4 Helen's mum and dad like *thinking* / *doing things*.
5 Helen thinks her mum and dad *understand* / *don't understand* her.
6 The taxi office is *behind* / *below* the flat.
7 Helen's room is *cold* / *hot*.
8 Helen's hands feel *cold* / *hot*.

3 Put the sentences in order.
1 Helen closes her eyes. ☐
2 Helen is a bed. ☐
3 Helen hears a voice in her head. ☐
4 Helen's head and hands feel hot. ☐
5 Helen gets into bed. ☐
6 Auntie Carol is working in the office. ☐1☐
7 Helen's hands are yellow. ☐
8 Helen doesn't want to talk to Auntie Carol. ☐

4 Are the sentences true (*T*) or false (*F*)?

1 Helen isn't dark. ☐T☐
2 Helen's mum and dad work in a taxi office. ☐
3 Auntie Carol drives a taxi. ☐
4 People call for a taxi and Helen's mum and dad answer the phone. ☐
5 Helen likes Auntie Carol. ☐
6 Helen's room is cold. ☐
7 Helen hears a voice in her head and knows who is talking to her. ☐
8 Helen doesn't know how she becomes a bed. ☐

5 Answer the questions.

1 What does Helen like doing?

....

2 Why doesn't Helen want to talk to Auntie Carol?

....

3 Why isn't Helen cold in her room?

....

4 What is very strange?

....

LOOKING FORWARD

6 Tick (✓) what you think happens in the next two chapters.

1 The bed changes back into Helen. ☐
2 Helen knows who is talking to her. ☐
3 Helen becomes things. ☐

Chapter 3

A bag, a book and a chair

I am the bed and the bed is me.

The door opens. Auntie Carol comes into my room. 'Helen?' she says. 'Are you in here?'

She looks at the bed, but she can't see me.

She leaves the room. I can hear her. 'Helen! Helen!' Then I hear the voice again.

'You can be Helen again now,' the voice tells me. 'Just think, "I want to be Helen."'

'I don't want to be the bed now,' I think. 'I want to be Helen again.'

Then I am. I'm me again. I'm Helen again – I'm not the bed.

Auntie Carol comes back into my room. 'You *are* here,' she says.

She looks at me. 'Helen? Are you OK?'

'Yes,' I say. I'm not OK of course. But I can't tell Auntie Carol. I can't say, 'Auntie Carol, I can *be* a bed!'

I find the baby blanket and look at it for a long time. Then I hear the voice again.

'You can be anything you want to be,' it tells me.

'Who are you?' I ask the voice.

But the voice doesn't answer my question.

The next day I look at Mum's bag. I look at it and I think, 'I am the bag. I *am* the bag.'

My head goes hot and my hands go yellow. Then I become[4] the bag. Mum takes me to work with her. She doesn't know the bag is me.

21

I try with it with a book. I become a book and a boy reads me.

Then I try it with a chair. I become a chair and Dad sits on me! I can become anything, but … how? And why?

On Saturday afternoon Mum and Dad are working. Auntie Carol and I are in the taxi office. She gets a phone call about her son. My cousin Jack is not well.

'I must go,' she tells me. 'Your mum's coming back in five minutes. I'm sorry to leave you alone[5] in the office, Helen.'

'That's OK,' I say.

'Good girl,' Auntie Carol says, and she goes.

I wait for Mum in the taxi office. Then I hear a noise. Is it Mum? I'm going to shout to her, but then I hear a man.

'In here!' he says.

Who is he? Something's wrong. I must call the police.

Chapter 4

Yellow money

'In here!' the man says again. He's near now.

I put my hand on the phone to call the police, but two men come in. One is tall and one is short.

The tall man has a gun.

'Put the phone down,' he tells me.

I do it.

'Where's the money?' asks the short man.

'The money's in a box next to the computer,' I tell the men.

'Get it,' says the tall man.

I look at the gun. I want Mum to come.

'It's OK,' says the voice in my head. 'I'm here.' I'm very happy to hear the voice again.

I get the box with the money.

'Now open it!' the tall man shouts at me.

I open the box. I don't like the man shouting at me. I feel angry. And very hot.

'Look!' says the short man. 'Her hands are yellow!'

I put my hands on the money. 'I am the money!' I think. 'I *am* the money!' And then I am.

'Where is she?' asks the tall man. He looks for me.

'I don't know,' says his friend. 'But I don't like it here!'

'No,' says the tall man. 'Something's very strange.' He takes the box with the money and they leave. I am the money. I go with them.

They run out and get in their car. The tall man drives. The short man has the box.

He opens it and looks at the money. He's looking at me, but he doesn't know it.

'Look at all this, Joe!' he says.
Joe laughs. 'Yeah!' he says. 'We're rich, Frank!

Joe is driving fast. The money comes out of the box into the car. *I* come out of the box into the car.

'You can *be* the car!' the voice in my head tells me.

Yes! 'I am the car!' I think. 'I *am* the car!'

'The money's yellow!' Frank says.

'What?' says Joe.

'I *am* the car!' I think again.

And then I am. And I know what to do.

LOOKING BACK

1 Check your answers to *Looking forward* on page 19.

ACTIVITIES

2 <u>Underline</u> the correct words in each sentence.

1 Auntie Carol looks at the bed and *sees* / <u>*doesn't see*</u> Helen.

2 Helen tells Auntie Carol that she *is* / *isn't* OK.

3 Helen becomes a book and *a boy* / *her dad* reads her.

4 Helen becomes a chair and her *mum* / *dad* sits on her.

5 Helen is waiting for her *mum* / *dad* in the taxi office.

6 Helen *calls* / *doesn't call* the police.

7 Helen *becomes* / *doesn't become* the money.

8 The short man looks at the money. He *knows* / *doesn't know* that Helen is the money.

9 Helen *becomes* / *doesn't become* the car.

3 Answer the questions.

In Chapters 3 and 4, who ...

1 goes into Helen's room? *Auntie Carol*

2 looks at the baby blanket for a long time? ....

3 takes a bag to work? ....

4 isn't well? ....

5 waits in the taxi office? ....

6 is angry? ....

7 drives a car? ....

8 opens the money box and looks at all the money? ....

4 Put the sentences in order.

1 Helen is a chair. ☐

2 Helen doesn't call the police. ☐

3 Helen is angry. ☐

4 Helen is alone in the taxi office. ☐

5 Auntie Carol doesn't see Helen in her room. ☐1

6 Helen and the men get in the car. ☐

7 Helen is a book. ☐

8 Helen's mum doesn't know Helen is the bag. ☐

5 Answer the questions.

1 Where does Helen's mum take her?

....

2 What does Helen want to do at the start of Chapter 4?

....

3 What things does Helen become in Chapters 3 and 4?

....

LOOKING FORWARD

6 Tick (✓) what you think happens in the final chapters.

1 Helen drives to the police station. ☐

2 Helen doesn't hear the voice in her head again. ☐

3 Helen helps people. ☐

Chapter 5

At the police station

I am the car. I drive up a road to the right.

'The car!' shouts Joe. 'Something's wrong! We don't want to go up this road!'

I stop. The men look out.

'We're at the police station!' says Frank. 'Quick! We mustn't stop here!'

'I can't start the car!' shouts Joe.

'We must get out!' shouts Frank.

He tries to open the door. He can't open it.

'Open the doors!' he shouts at his friend.

Joe tries again. 'I can't!' he says.

I am the car and I can make a big noise. I make it.

'What's that?' asks Frank.

'It's the car alarm[6]' Joe shouts.
'Stop it!' Frank shouts.
'I can't!'

There is lots of noise. After a minute, a policeman comes out of the police station.

The policeman looks in one of my windows.

'Stop the noise, please,' he says to Joe.

'These men are bad!' I want to tell the policeman. 'They've got our money!' But cars can't talk. For a minute I don't know what to do.

The noise doesn't stop.

'Open the door please,' says the policeman to Joe.

'I can't!' Joe says. He's shouting at the policeman now. He's angry and he wants to get out of the car. He takes his gun out. He hits[7] the window with it. He hits *me* with it, because I am the car. Ow!

'I don't want to be the car now!' I think quickly. 'I want to be Helen!'

'The car's yellow!' Frank says. 'I don't like this! I want to get out!'

I'm Helen again. The men look at me. Their mouths are open. They don't understand.

'How—?' one of them starts to say, but I quickly open the window and shout at the policeman.

'Help!' I shout.

The gun is in Joe's hand. It's near my face now. I'm looking at it.

'Put the gun down,' the policeman says from the street.

'Put your hands up!' Joe shouts at the policeman. His face is red and his eyes are big.

'What is Joe going to do?' I think. 'What is he going to do?'

Chapter 6

My new job

'Joe,' Frank says. 'She's just a girl!'

The policeman has his hands up. 'Please, sir,' he says. 'Give me the gun and get out of the car.'

I hear the voice in my head. 'You can *be* Frank,' it says. 'Try to get near him.'

I look at Frank. 'Help me,' I ask him. 'Please.'

He puts a hand on my shoulder. I know he doesn't want me to die.

'Joe, please!' he says again.

'Shut up[8], Frank!' Joe shouts.

'I am Frank,' I think. 'I *am* Frank!' And then I am. I am Frank.

'Where's the girl?' Joe asks. His mouth is open again. It's very easy to take the gun from his hand.

'Hey!' says Joe. 'What are you doing?'

Then I open the car door and give the gun to the policeman. I talk in Frank's voice.

'Look in the car,' I tell him. 'There's some money in there. It isn't our money. It's from the taxi office.'

The policeman looks in the car. He sees the box and the money.

'I don't want to be Frank now,' I think. 'I want to be Helen.'

Then I am Helen again and Frank is standing next to me. He doesn't look well.

'Where am I?' Frank asks.

'Come with me, please,' the policeman says to Joe and Frank.

He looks at me too. I know he doesn't understand. 'You too, please,' he says.

The police phone Mum and Dad. They bring a film from the taxi office. We watch it.

We can see the two men with the gun on the TV. The policeman stops the film.

'Thank you,' he says to Mum and Dad. Then he takes[9] the two men away.

When we're at the taxi office, I tell Mum and Dad everything.

Mum and Dad look at me.

'Is it true[10]?' Mum asks me.

'Yes,' I say. 'I think I'm here to help. The police. The world. Anyone who wants my help.'

The voice is in my head again.

'Yes,' it says. 'Yes, that's right. You are here to help people.'

'Who are you?' I want to ask. 'Are you my birth parents?'

But I don't say anything. Because my adoptive parents are here with me. They hold me in their arms.

I kiss them. I'm happy.

'I love you,' I tell them.

'We love you too,' they tell me.

OK, I think that's everything. That's my story. It's true, all of it. I'm just a girl – when I'm not a bag or money or a car.

But listen, I must go. Look over there! A man is trying to take an old woman's bag! I must make a quick change. I've got to help her!

Goodbye for now!

LOOKING BACK

1 Check your answers to *Looking forward* on page 31.

ACTIVITIES

2 Put the sentences in order.
1 Joe can't open the car window. ☐
2 Helen takes the gun from Joe's hand. ☐
3 Helen stops being the car. ☐
4 Helen tells her mum and dad everything. ☐
5 Helen and the men stop at the police station. ☑
6 Helen's mum and dad bring a film from the taxi office. ☐
7 Helen becomes Frank. ☐
8 The car alarm makes a big noise. ☐

3 Match the questions with the answers.
1 Who is in the car? ☑ d
2 Where does Helen stop? ☐
3 Why does a policeman come out of the police station? ☐
4 Who hits Helen? ☐
5 Who is happy? ☐

a He hears the car alarm.
b Joe.
c Helen.
d Helen, Joe and Frank.
e The police station.

46

4 Are the sentences true (*T*) or false (*F*)?

1 Joe drives the car. $\boxed{F}$
2 Joe can't stop the noise. ☐
3 Joe opens the door for the policeman. ☐
4 Helen takes the gun from Joe's hand. ☐
5 Helen phones her mum and dad. ☐
6 The policeman takes the men away. ☐
7 Helen wants to help people. ☐
8 Helen's mum and dad kiss her. ☐

5 <u>Underline</u> the correct words in each sentence.

1 The car stops at the <u>*police station*</u> / *taxi office*.
2 Joe hits *Helen* / *the policeman* with a gun.
3 The policeman looks for the money in the *car* / *taxi office*.
4 Helen's *adoptive parents* / *birth parents* hold her in their arms.
5 Helen is going to help *an old woman* / *a man*.

6 Answer the questions.

1 Who does Helen become?

....

2 What does the policeman see on the film?

....

3 Where does Helen tell her mum and dad everything?

....

Glossary

[1]**adoptive daughter** (page 6)   the daughter of parents that are not her biological or birth parents

[2]**voice** (page 17) *noun*   the noise that you make when you speak or sing

[3]**strange** (page 17) *adjective*   something that is not usual

[4]**become** (page 21) *verb*   to start to be something

[5]**alone** (page 25) *adjective*   without any other people

[6]**alarm** (page 34) *noun*   a big noise that tells you there is danger or something bad

[7]**hit** (page 35) *verb*   to try and hurt somebody or something because you are angry

[8]**shut up** (page 39) *phrasal verb*   to stop speaking or making a noise

[9]**take away** (page 42) *phrasal verb*   to make somebody leave a place and go with you

[10]**true** (page 42) *adjective*   something that is real, not false